ORANGUTAN BABY

What are orangutans?

❖   Orangutans are mammals.

❖   Every night, an orangutan will bend tree branches to make a nest for sleeping.

❖   Orangutans mostly live in trees.

Where do Orangutans live?

❖   Orangutans live in tropical rain forests in Asia.

What do Orangutans eat?

❖   Orangutans eat nuts, bark, fruit, and other parts of plants

❖   Sometimes they eat insects, too.

Did You Know?

A group of orangutans is called a congress (Kong-gris).

KITTEN

What are Kittens?

- ❖ Kittens are baby cats.
- ❖ They are mammals. They have fur on their bodies.

What do Kittens eat?

- ❖ Kittens drink milk from their mothers.
- ❖ They can eat soft kitten food after three weeks.

Cat Names:

- ❖ A group of kittens is called a Kindle.
- ❖ A girl cat is called a queen.
- ❖ A boy cat is called a tomcat.

Did You Know?

Kittens and cats do not have eyelashes.

PIGLET

What are piglets?

❖ Piglets are baby pigs.

❖ They are mammals. They have stiff hair on their bodies.

❖ Piglets can be brown, black, pink, or white.

Where do piglets live?

❖ Piglets live all over the world. Many people keep them on farms.

❖ Piglets do not live in Antarctica. It is too cold!

What do piglets eat?

❖ Piglets eat plants.

❖ They also eat small animals, like worms and snakes.

Pig Names:

❖ A group of piglets is called a litter.

❖ Girl pigs are called sows.

❖ Boy pigs are called boars.

LION CUB

What are lions?

- ❖ Lions are mammals.
- ❖ Lions are large cats.
- ❖ Boy lions have hair around their heads. This hair is called a mane.
- ❖ Lions have long tails.

Where do lions live?

- ❖ Lions live on savannas in Africa, Asia, and India.
- ❖ They are found in zoos around the world, too.

What do lions eat?

- ❖ Lions eat meat.
- ❖ They hunt other large animals. They like to eat wildebeests, zebras, buffalo, wild boar, and deer.

Lion Names

- ❖ Boy lions are called lions.
- ❖ Girl lions are called lionesses.
- ❖ Baby lions are called cubs.
- ❖ A group of lions is called a pride.

FAWN

What are fawns?

❖ Fawns are baby deer.

❖ They are mammals. They have fur on their bodies.

❖ Fawns are born with white spots on their fur.
The spots go away after about a year.

Where do fawns live?

❖ Fawns and grown-up deer live all around the world.
They are not found in Antarctica or Australia.

❖ They live in forests and on savannas.

What do fawns eat?

❖ Fawns drink milk from their mothers.

❖ They also eat leaves, grass, twigs, and fruit.

Deer Names:

❖ Boy deer are called bucks.

❖ Girl deer are called does (dohz).

❖ Baby deer are called fawns.

PENGUIN CHICK

What are penguins?

- ❖ Penguins are birds. They have feathers on their bodies.
- ❖ They also have webbed feet.
- ❖ Penguins cannot fly, but they are great swimmers.

Where do penguins live?

- ❖ Penguins live in Antarctica. It is very cold there!
- ❖ They also live in parts of South America, Africa, New Zealand, and Australia!

What do penguins eat?

- ❖ Penguins eat fish, squid, and krill.

Penguin Names:

- ❖ A group of penguins is called a rookery (ROOK-er-ee).
- ❖ A baby penguin is called a chick.

Did You Know?

Penguins slide on the ice on their bellies.

PANDA CUB

What Are Pandas?

❖ Pandas are mammals. They are a kind of bear.

❖ Pandas have black and white fur on their bodies.

❖ These bears have thick and heavy bones.

Where Do Pandas Live?

❖ Pandas live in damp forests in southwestern China.

What Do Pandas Eat?

❖ Pandas eat a plant called bamboo.

Did You Know?

A mother panda takes care of her baby for about two years.

PUPPY

What are puppies?

- ❖ A puppy is a baby dog.
- ❖ They are mammals. They have fur on their bodies.
- ❖ Puppies can be many colors. Their fur can be brown, black, white, gray, or mixed.
- ❖ Puppies can have spots, too.

What do puppies eat?

- ❖ Puppies drink milk from their mothers.
- ❖ They can eat dry puppy food when they are four weeks old.

Did You Know?

Puppies are born blind, deaf, and toothless.

ELEPHANT CALF

What Is an Elephant?

❖ Elephants are mammals.

❖ There are two kinds of elephants: African and Asian.

❖ Elephants have thick skin that is covered with short, coarse hair.

Where Do Elephants Live?

❖ African elephants live in savannas and woodlands in Africa.

❖ Asian elephants live in the scrub forests of India, Nepal, and Southeast Asia.

What Do Elephants Eat?

❖ Elephants eat grass, fruit, leaves, and bark.

❖ Wild elephants eat 300 to 400 pounds every day!

❖ They also drink about 20 gallons of water.

Did You Know?

Elephants flap their large ears to keep cool.

OWLET

What Are Owlets?

❖ Owlets are baby owls. Owls are birds.

❖ They have feathers on their bodies.

❖ Owls even have thick feathers on their feet.
This protects them from snake and rat bites.

Where Do Owlets Live?

❖ Owlets are found on every continent except Antarctica.

What Do Owlets Eat?

❖ Owlets are carnivores. They eat rodents, insects,
and frogs. Owls eat the entire animal. Then they
throw up the hair, teeth, and bones in a small chunk
called a pellet.

Did You Know?

An owl cannot move its eyes within their sockets.
The bird has to turn its entire head to look around.

LAMB

What are lambs?
- ❖ Lambs are baby sheep.
- ❖ They are mammals.
- ❖ They have stiff hair on their bodies called wool.

Where do lambs live?
- ❖ Lambs live on farms.
- ❖ Sheep and lambs are raised for their wool. Wool is used to make things like clothes and blankets.

What do lambs eat?
- ❖ Lambs drink milk from their mothers.
- ❖ They also eat grass and small plants.

Sheep Names:
- ❖ Boy sheep are called bucks.
- ❖ Girl sheep are called ewes (YOOz).
- ❖ Baby sheep are called lambs.

SEA TURTLE HATCHLING

What Is a Sea Turtle?

- ❖ Sea turtles are reptiles. They are excellent swimmers and divers.
- ❖ These animals range in size from two to six feet long.
- ❖ Sea turtles have a hard shell on their backs. The shell is made up of plates called scutes (SKOOTES).

Where Do Sea Turtles Live?

- ❖ Sea turtles are found in warm oceans around the world.

What Do Sea Turtles Eat?

- ❖ Sea turtles eat crabs, lobster, shrimp, shellfish, sea jellies, sea grass, and algae.

Did You Know?

Female (girl) sea turtles go back to the beach where they were born to lay their eggs.

HEDGEHOG PUP

What Is a Hedgehog?

- ❖ Hedgehogs are mammals.
- ❖ A hedgehog has spines on its back. The spines are stiff and spiky.
- ❖ Hedgehogs have soft white hair on their bellies.

Where Do Hedgehogs Live?

- ❖ Hedgehogs are found in deserts and forests in Africa, Asia, Europe, and New Zealand.

What Do Hedgehogs Eat?

- ❖ Hedgehogs are known as insectivores. This means they eat insects.
- ❖ They also eat snails, mice, lizards, snakes, eggs, and dead animals.

Hedgehog Names

- ❖ A girl hedgehog is called a sow.
- ❖ A boy hedgehog is called a boar.
- ❖ A baby hedgehog is called a piglet or a pup.

Image © Istock

WOLF PUP

What Is a Wolf?

- ❖ A wolf is a mammal. It has fur on its body.
- ❖ Wolves live in groups with other members of their family. These groups are called packs.
- ❖ All of the wolves in a pack help to take care of the pups.

Where Do Wolves Live?

- ❖ Wolf pups live in wilderness areas in North America, northern Europe, and Asia.

What Do Wolves Eat?

- ❖ Wolf pups, like adult wolves, are carnivores. They eat goats, sheep, deer, birds, mice, and other animals that the adults kill. The adults eat and then throw up some of the food for the pups.

Did You Know?

Wolves have excellent eyesight, hearing, and sense of smell.

KOALA JOEY

What Is a Koala?

- ❖ Koalas are mammals. They are also marsupials (mar-SOOP-ee-uls).
- ❖ Koalas have stiff fur on their bodies.
- ❖ These animals have two thumbs on their hands to help them climb trees.

Where Do Koalas Live?

- ❖ Koalas are found in eucalyptus (YOO-Ka-LIP-tiss) trees in southeastern and eastern Australia.

What Do Koalas Eat?

- ❖ Koalas eat the leaves of the eucalyptus tree.

Did You Know?

A baby Koala is called a joey. When a joey is born, it is only the size of a jellybean!

Image © Istock

SKUNK PUP

What Is a Skunk?

- ❖ Skunks are mammals. They have black and white fur on their bodies.
- ❖ These animals can spray a smelly liquid. They use the spray to keep predators away.
- ❖ Skunks are nocturnal (nok-TERN-ul). This means that they are active at night.

Where Do Skunks Live?

- ❖ Skunks live in wooded areas in North, Central, and South America.

What Do Skunks Eat?

- ❖ Skunks eat small mammals, rodents, reptiles, insects, worms, eggs, fish, plants, and fruit.

Did You Know?

Skunks can spray predators up to 10 feet (3 m) away!

Image © Istock